DENNIS

Pat Kennett

WORLD TRUCKS NO 6

Patrick Stephens, Cambridge

Also in the same series and by the same author

No 1: ERF
No 2: Scania
No 3: Seddon Atkinson
No 4: MAN
No 5: Daf

First published in 1979

Not for distribution in North America

Acknowledgement
The author would like to thank the National Motor Museum for providing the photographs which appear on the following pages: front endpaper, 13, 14 bottom, 15, 16, 17, 21 middle and bottom, 25, 26 bottom, 27 bottom, 29 bottom, 32 bottom, 33 bottom, 35 inset and 36 top.

British Library Cataloguing in Publication Data

Kennett, Pat
  World trucks.
  No. 6 : Dennis
  1. Motor-trucks - History
  I. Title
  629.22'4'0904   TL230

  ISBN 0 85059 328 X

Set in 10 on 10pt Baskerville type by Stevenage Printing Ltd, Stevenage. Printed on 100 gsm Buccaneer II Matt coated cartridge paper and bound in Great Britain by The Garden City Press Ltd, Letchworth, for the publishers, Patrick Stephens Limited, Bar Hill, Cambridge, CB3 8EL, England.

CONTENTS

AUTHOR'S PREFACE

Once again in a World Trucks volume, the problems of condensing the activities of a prolific and inventive manufacturer which began life before the turn of the century, into a modest book with less than one hundred pages, have been immense. The Scania volume posed such a problem, and this book about the famous Dennis company of Guildford involved me in even greater difficulties. Some idea of the size of the task of sorting out all the facts and then selecting those which, it is hoped, would make a representative story, can be gained from the fact that over two hundred different types of fire engine alone are recorded among the Dennis product files, and many of those had several versions specially built for individual customers. Then there were the innumerable bus variants in the first quarter of this century, and in later years the trucks and municipal vehicles in great quantity and variety, all adding up to a tremendous inventory of fascinating vehicles. Consequently I beg forgiveness if any reader's particular interest within Dennis is given scant coverage, or even no coverage at all.

What I have set out to do is to convey the spirit and motivation that established the modest workshop in Guildford as a major commercial vehicle power as the years rolled by, and furthermore I have outlined the major engineering developments that characterised the splendid vehicles that made such an enviable reputation for Dennis, and to some extent the whole British vehicle industry. Much of their design was unique, and some of it well before its logical time. For example, a speaker at an important conference at the time of the 1978 Motor Show asserted that the time had come for transmissions which freewheeled their countershafts in order to improve truck fuel consumptions. He was somewhat surprised to learn that Dennis had had just such a design almost 70 years earlier. I have also attempted to draw a picture of the changing fortunes at Dennis, which led to the takeover by Hestair, and the happy outcome of that move, which has re-established the old Guildford company as a major exporter of heavy vehicles.

In my lengthy researches, I was enthusiastically aided by numerous friends and colleagues. Among those, special mention should be made of the help given by Nick Georgano and his staff at the Library of the National Motor Museum, and John Dennis, Phil Pearce and Tom Realff at the Dennis works, all of whom had great funds of data and recollections of the company's former activity. I also must thank Len Poole who provided innumerable suggestions and leads for me to follow in the course of the research work.

A curious fact emerged during all that enquiry work, and that was although the early decades of Dennis's work were fairly well recorded and illustrated, material and records of more recent years, particularly the post-war years, were relatively scarce. Clearly the notion was abroad that current activity did not constitute historical record, and now some twenty or thirty years later it is difficult to fill in the details accurately. That reinforces my assertion that today's routine is tomorrow's historical record, and perhaps I might appeal to anyone and everyone involved in industry to avoid the temptation to discard current or just-obsolete records. One day they will be valuable documents.

Despite the limitations of recording over eighty years of automobile engineering in just about as many pages, I trust that my readers will welcome this book in the World Trucks series. The subject is rather different in character from those of any Scania or MAN, but nevertheless, the tale is a fascinating one, and one which I hope will bring a measure of enjoyment.

Pat Kennett

THE WEST-COUNTRY BOYS

The name of Dennis Brothers is irrevocably associated with the town of Guildford, in the sleepy, leafy countryside to the south-west of London, but John Dennis and his brother Raymond were west-country men. They were brought up in the tiny Devon village of Huntsham, in a farming community, but John in particular could not raise very much enthusiasm for farming. He was far more interested in machinery than livestock or crops. Somewhat against his family's wishes, he took an apprenticeship with an ironmonger in Bideford, which was then the busiest market town in north Devon. An ironmonger of that period did not simply sell tools and hardware, like his namesake of a century later, but was a versatile engineer, who had to be capable of making or repairing almost anything made of metal, from cooking pots to farm machinery, tools to bicycles.

Even so, John Cawsey Dennis, having almost completed his apprenticeship, was restless. He felt there must be more to life than tinkering around with sundry bits of machinery in a sleepy west-country town, and in any case there was no guarantee that he would be given a proper job once his apprenticeship was complete. He saw an advertisement in a trade magazine by a firm called Filmer and Mason, who wanted an assistant in their ironmonger's business in a place called Guildford. A map from his family bookshelf told John that Guildford was about 175 miles away, not far from London, it seemed from far-off Devon. Without telling his family what he was about, he caught the train eastwards early one morning in the summer of 1894, went for an interview at Filmer and Masons, and got the job.

His family were far from happy about what he had done when they finally found out, but John was a lot happier than he had been in the west. Things were much more alive in this part of the world, more up to date. In between his work at Filmer and Mason, John thought he would build himself a bicycle, and by

purchasing parts one or two at a time, mainly from his employers, he completed the machine in a few weeks. Having done that, he had spent his meagre savings and had no money left at all, so he persuaded a friendly tailor in High Street, Guildford to exhibit the machine along with the cloth in his window, advertising it for sale. Within two days, the splendidly built and finished cycle was sold. John Dennis was solvent again, and he had made a nice profit over and above what he had spent to build that first machine. If he could do it once, he pondered, why not do it again, and again? Why not indeed? And so it was that John Dennis found himself building bicycles on a regular basis, even though he was still working for Filmer and Mason.

The next step was to find out more about parts' supplies and manufacture, because even he, a humble west-country boy, could clearly see that the people he bought them from were making a good profit, and their suppliers did not make the parts. So there were a lot of 'margins' in his prices long before he got hold of the parts for assembly. Consequently, he went to work for a time with Brown Brothers, the famous parts factors, who still trade under the same name, to learn about the world of manufacture and supply of machined engineering components. With that essential education behind him, he returned to Guildford, where he had many friends, and set up 'The Universal Athletic Stores' at 94, High Street. The main object of that somewhat grandiosely named establishment was to build and sell bicycles although it stocked other sports gear too. Within a matter of a few days he had his first two models, the 'Speed King' for gentlemen, and 'Speed Queen' for ladies, on show.

His production facility was, to say the least, primitive. It consisted of a pear tree in the small garden behind the shop, from the branches of which John would suspend a frame with a rope sling, and then set about assembling all the pieces on to it. He had negotiated good prices with Brown Brothers, and the venture was an immediate success. That was in January 1895, and so enthused was John about his new business, and so busy did he become, that he wrote and asked his younger brother Herbert Raymond to come and help. John himself was still only 24 years old, and his brother a mere lad of 17, but together they made their little cycle business prosper. A unique service offered by the Dennis brothers to their customers was detailed instruction in how to look after and maintain their cycles properly, and they even ran classes for non-riders in the art of cycling, so making new customers for themselves.

By the summer of 1896 the pear tree was a woefully inadequate 'factory' and a modest but well equipped workshop was built behind the shop, where production could be continued whatever the weather or time of day. At that time, what we now call 'public relations exercises' were almost unknown, but the brothers Dennis knew a thing or two about the subject, even if they had never heard the term. Their shop had got off to a good start because they organised a competition, with a cycle lamp as a prize, in which contestants had to estimate how long the wheel of an upturned bicycle in the window would revolve, having been spun vigorously by the president of Guildford Cycle Club. In fact the wheel spun for over 12 minutes — an indication of the excellence of the product — and its slowly decreasing progress was watched anxiously by a large crowd, and the event made the local newspapers.

When the Jubilee of Queen Victoria was celebrated across the length and breadth of the country in 1897, the Dennis brothers made a most peculiar machine. It was a cycle of a kind, but with a pyramid frame nearly ten feet tall, atop which an intrepid rider dressed as Mephistopheles propelled the contraption by means of a very long chain. It bore no advertising, but in Guildford's Jubilee parade it towered above everything else and everyone knew where it had come from. By that time, assembly of 'bought out' parts had given way to actual manufacture, firstly of simple parts like spindles and brackets, and eventually the whole machine. They took a stand at the important National Cycle Exhibition at Crystal Palace in 1897, and the construction and design of the machine as a whole, and details like a pneumatic saddle, won the little Guildford concern widespread acclaim. Not satisfied with such successes, Raymond Dennis rode their cycles in races and his numerous awards in that field won yet more business for the High Street shop.

Business expanded to such an extent that the old pear tree had to be cut down to make way for a properly built workshop for cycle manufacture, and with about 1,000 sq ft of workspace, the Dennis brothers had their first factory, complete with plating and enamelling equipment, numerous small machines, all powered by a Crossley gas engine. With such a facility at their disposal, and fully paid for too, attention turned for the first time to powered vehicles.

The first experiment involved a tricycle, fitted with a single-cylinder De Dion engine — an already well known French-made power unit — which was adapted to fit on the rear of a strengthened frame. A certain amount of experimenting was needed in matters like sprocket sizes, and wheels to accept the higher weight and speed of the powered machine had to be specially developed. But by the summer of 1899, they had a satisfactory tricycle, which ran very well indeed. So well in fact that John Dennis was spotted by one Sergeant Hall doing an alleged 16 mph *up* the High Street in Guildford which has a gradient exceeding nine per cent, and was in due course fined 20 shillings for 'riding furiously'. The instinctive ability to turn adversity into profit once again showed itself, and advertisements shortly appeared in *The Autocar Journal* and in newspapers proclaiming that the new Dennis motor tricycle would climb Guildford High Street at 16 mph 'on sworn testimony of a Constable of the Law'.

The motor tricycle was an immediate success, and sold readily. To that model was added a series of four-wheeled motor vehicles, which were not quite motor cars, but were built on cycle-engineering lines and called 'quadricycles'. Some years later, in a publication of 1910 aimed at establishing a certain amount of long-term experience for the company, a drawing appeared of a quadricycle or car as it was called, said to have been made in 1895 by the Dennis Brothers. Whether it was actually made, or was a figment of someone's over-fertile imagination, is not clear. But certainly there was no recorded sale of such a vehicle, nor indeed any mention in a catalogue, until 1900. However, by then the little Dennis vehicles had become very well known, not least by their successes in speed trials and competitions, as often as not ridden by the intrepid Raymond.

Such methods of advertising a product were popular at that time, and for many years to follow, and many manufacturers, among them Morgan, Godfrey, Nash and others well known in the motoring field, piloted their own machines to competition success as a prelude, it was hoped, to commercial success. De Dion engines were still used by Dennis, usually the 2.75 hp single-cylinder unit, which was stepped up to a genuine 3 hp by Dennis modifications to the cylinder head and carburettor. Despite the successes of the cycle-engineered machines, it seemed to the brothers that there was more future in a proper motor car than in the tubular-framed devices that they had built up to the turn of the century.

As the new year and the new century began, so work started on a real motor car for the first time, using a great deal of the experience gained in developing and building the old tricycles and quadricycles. Perhaps the most important lesson learned as the Dennis boys competed against many other makes in trials and shows, was that of the innumerable firms attempting to make their own power units, very few enjoyed any degree of success. They consequently made up their minds to continue to use a proprietary engine, and concentrate on chassis developments only 'for the time being'. In fact it was not until many years later that the initial policy was changed. Consequently when the first cars appeared in the catalogue and on the roads in 1901, they had 8 hp single-cylinder De Dion engines.

These cars were built in a new workshop located in a disused army barracks in Guildford, but within little more than a year, those premises were abandoned as inadequate, and a fine new headquarters was established at Rodborough Buildings in Onslow Street. This was a substantial three storey, brick-constructed building, with ample access and lighting, and was an imposing place for such a young firm to have built. At that stage, they reorganised as a private limited liability company, with a capital of £30,000 subscribed by a small but enthusiastic body of Dennis customers and associates. Their support of Dennis Brothers Ltd was amply justified as dividends steadily grew from an initial modest five per cent in 1902 to a generous 12½ per cent by 1904.

Reliability was extremely suspect among many cars at that time, and the fear of constant breakdown was, it was felt, a major stumbling block to sales. So the Dennis brothers, aided by Reginald Downing who had recently joined them, entered their vehicles in long distance reliability trials which were organised by the Automobile Club of Great Britain and Ireland, later to become the RAC. The first was a modest 60-mile affair from London to Oxford in 1902, which saw two Dennises driven by Raymond and Reg Downing, both of which did the run non-stop. Next came a 1,000-mile trial, which was completed by both Dennis entries without difficulty, while cars were entered in the Tourist Trophy race, held at the time in the Isle of Man, and although they did not win the race they both finished creditably.

A wide range of cars was quickly developed, including 12 and 14 hp touring models, 16 and 20 hp town cars and limousines, a big brougham and a cab version too. At the 1903 Motor Show at Crystal Palace, almost £30,000 worth of cars were sold off the stand, and orders taken for many more.

It was in that year that the technical innovation began to appear which marked Dennis engineering for a long time. One feature was the 'spring drive', a torsional shock absorber device at the input end of the transmission to smooth drive line shocks. The other was a worm type final drive, patented by Dennis for vehicle use. The worm drive was a source of great and sometimes acrimonious debate. Those who used bevel drive accused the worm of being inefficient, non-reversible and heavy, when in fact it was none of these things. It had, on the other hand, extraordinary durability even under rough treatment, and remained a Dennis feature for many years. Dennis even built a worm-drive racing car, powered by a 40 hp Simms engine, but although it ran in sprints and speed trials in 1903, it never competed in the Gordon Bennet races for which it was built.

By 1907, not only was there a wide range of cars, but they were of very advanced design, with four-speed gear boxes in most cases, some fitted with a top-gear freewheel which left the friction-producing layshaft in the gear box stationary while driving in top gear. Fully floating axles were used, wherein a drive shaft could be replaced without disturbing the bearings, and on some models there was open-shaft drive to the rear axle instead of the heavier torque tube design used on all the earlier worm-axle types.

All this high grade engineering and design innovation was, in the opinion of both John Dennis and Reg Downing, something of a waste as much of it went to amuse the gentry of the land, who could afford to have a motor car as much because it was fashionable as for any real purpose. How much more rewarding it would be, they thought, if they could direct their ingenuity where it would make a real contribution to the economy of the country.

Accordingly, they turned their attentions to the design of commercial vehicles and, towards the end of 1904, their first real commercial vehicle was built and exhibited at the Crystal Palace Show. It was a 15 cwt van with a two-cylinder De Dion engine of 12 hp, and of course it incorporated the now-famous worm drive. Not surprisingly there were a number of common design features carried over from the car chassis. But there was one new feature which was to be found on Dennis commercials for many years. That was a separate sub-frame inside the main chassis rails, on to which the engine and transmission and all the auxiliaries were mounted, the whole attached to the main chassis at two points well back on the frame and a third at the front. The idea of this design was to relieve the main frame of much of the stress arising from torque at engine mountings and the like, leaving it free to cope with its simple load-bearing task. Although not the simplest or lightest way to build a motor vehicle, it certainly paid dividends in terms of durability in service.

That first van aroused a great deal of interest, particularly as it went to work for the world-famous Harrods Ltd of Knightsbridge. Enquiries came flooding in and, by the spring of 1905, there were already more commercial vehicles being built than there were private passenger cars. Most of the early ones were similar to that Harrods prototype, some with single-cylinder 8 hp engines, still obtained from De Dion in France, and some with the 12 hp twin. It was a modest vehicle for a modest load capacity, compared with some of the more spectacular goods carriers being built around that time by firms like Foden, Straker, Thornycroft and Leyland. But it established for itself and its makers a first class reputation for working ability and above all

reliability—a most important factor in commercial operation.

It had taken ten years for John Dennis and his younger brother Raymond to develop their engineering expertise to an extent where they could break into that most difficult of all motor markets, that of the working commercial vehicle. But they had made it, and made it with considerable success. The future of their enterprise was therefore well defined and secure. They would become commercial vehicle specialists. Although their cars continued in production for some years—one winning the first-ever Dewar Trophy in 1907 for outstanding motoring achievement by completing the first RAC 4,000-mile trial without a hitch—these took second place to the commercials from 1905 onwards, and by 1913 car production ceased altogether. But a great deal was to happen at Dennis before that date.

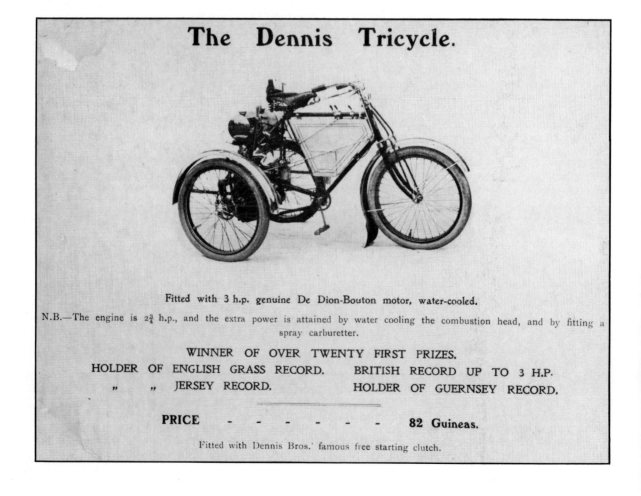

The Dennis Tricycle.

Fitted with 3 h.p. genuine De Dion-Bouton motor, water-cooled.

N.B.—The engine is 2¾ h.p., and the extra power is attained by water cooling the combustion head, and by fitting a spray carburetter.

WINNER OF OVER TWENTY FIRST PRIZES.

HOLDER OF ENGLISH GRASS RECORD.   BRITISH RECORD UP TO 3 H.P.

„   „   JERSEY RECORD.   HOLDER OF GUERNSEY RECORD.

PRICE   -   -   -   -   -   -   82 Guineas.

Fitted with Dennis Bros.' famous free starting clutch.

Left Catalogue page for the tricycle, dated 1899. This was the machine 'booked' for speeding up the hill in Guildford's High Street.

Above De Dion engines powered all three of these Dennis models photographed in 1901.

Right Driver's eye view of an early Dennis. The windscreen extends to waist-height only. The lever on the right operates the gearbox, with positive detents to keep it in gear.

DENNIS

The founders: John Cawsey Dennis **(left)** was born in 1871 and died just before the outbreak of war in 1939. **Far left** Raymond Dennis—later Sir Raymond, was seven years younger than his brother but died just a few weeks before John.

Below John Dennis takes his 1902 Dennis for a spin in the late summer of 1978. This car still starts first swing and runs quickly and reliably despite being more than 76 years old.

THE WEST-COUNTRY BOYS

Right The early worm axle case was divided on its centre line, as this view of the final drive of John Dennis's 1909 car shows. Later on, the worm assembly was mounted in a 'pot' which made assembly easier.

Below The 1909 Dennis splendidly preserved to this day. It sometimes covers several thousand miles a year on rallies and veteran vehicle events in the hands of John Dennis, the founder's grandson.

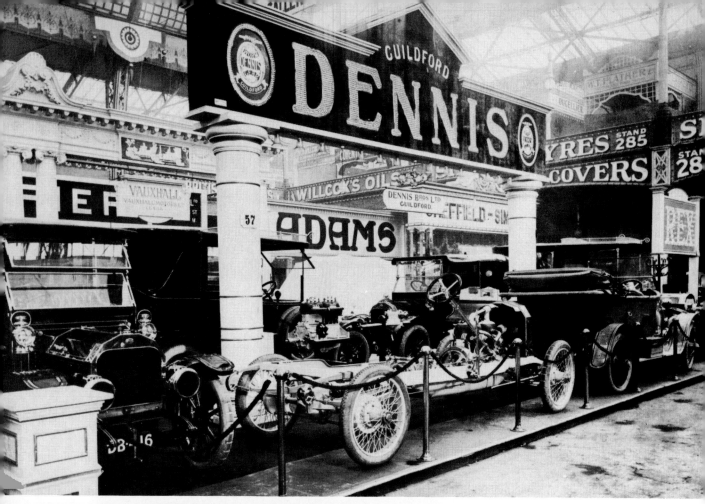

Above The Dennis stand at Crystal Palace in 1906 contained all kinds of cars and cabs, but no commercial vehicles.

Left The four-cylinder 24 hp engine of 1907-12 was typical of its period with cylinders cast in pairs and a T-head with inlet on the right. White and Poppe built these engines and others for Dennis.

Above right and right The original 1904 single-cylinder, De Dion-engined, 8 hp, 15 cwt chassis (top) was soon joined by a 12 hp, two-cylinder 1-tonner. From these modest machines the mighty Dennis commercials of the 1920s, '30s, '40s and '50s were sired.

Left Dennis broke into the booming world of commercial vehicles with a 15 cwt van model, and what better publicity could there have been than selling the first one to the prestigious house of Harrods in London?

Below The 1-ton, 12 hp van was a familiar sight among London traders as early as 1905. Driver protection was minimal.

Facing page 3-ton, 2-ton and 4-ton chassis of 1907-08 show similarities, including brass radiators, torque-reaction horn brackets, wooden wheels and four-cylinder Aster engines. Items like brake linkages and controls are almost identical.

Background photograph The 5-tonner was a big truck by any standards, and in 1907 when it was introduced it was a giant of rare proportions.

Inset The scene at Bristol's cattle market during the RAC's great commercial vehicle trials of 1907, which took the competitors to tests all over Britain. Dennis entries in the foreground are, left to right, the 30 cwt van, 3-ton van, 4-ton lorry and the medal winning 2-tonner partly visible. Thames and Straker Squire entries are seen behind.

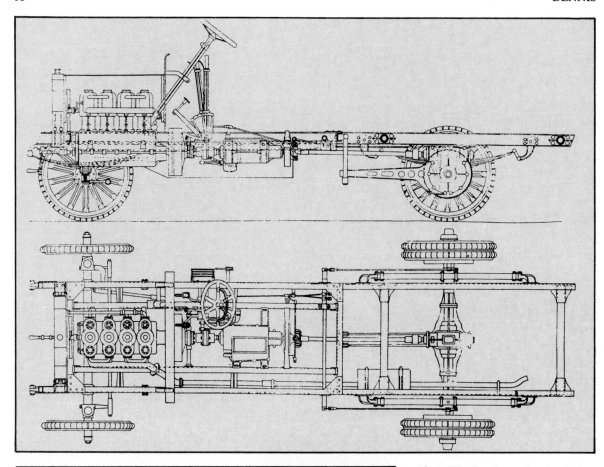

Above The first 2-ton chassis, similar to the type which competed in the great Commercial Vehicle Trials of 1907 followed typical Dennis practice with the power train mounted on a sub-frame. A 20 hp Aster engine powered the chassis at that stage.

Left Three of the many medals won in the early years of Dennis. They are from left to right: Passenger comfort award for town carriages, 1905: Award for flexibility of performance in the 1908 Crystal Palace Trials: Class award for covered vans, RAC commercial vehicle trials 1907.

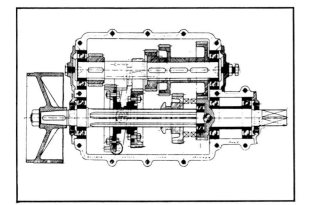

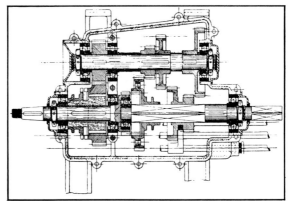

Above and right Details of Dennis gearboxes and axles, as supplied in 1910-11 on buses, trucks and fire engines.

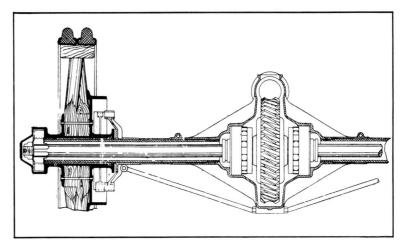

Below Layout sketch of the original Dennis turbine fire appliances show the big four-cylinder engine, the power-take-off drive to the rear mounted 300 gpm pump, the emergency water tank and the worm-drive axle. The early appliances had 40 hp engines but versions with 60 hp or even 100 hp were built, especially for export orders.

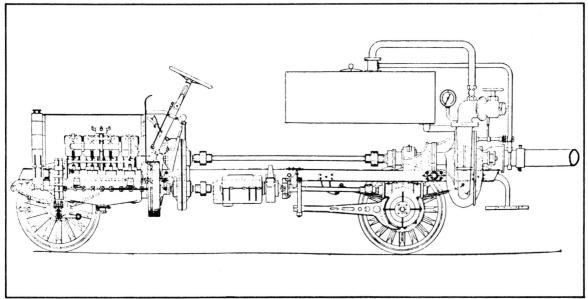

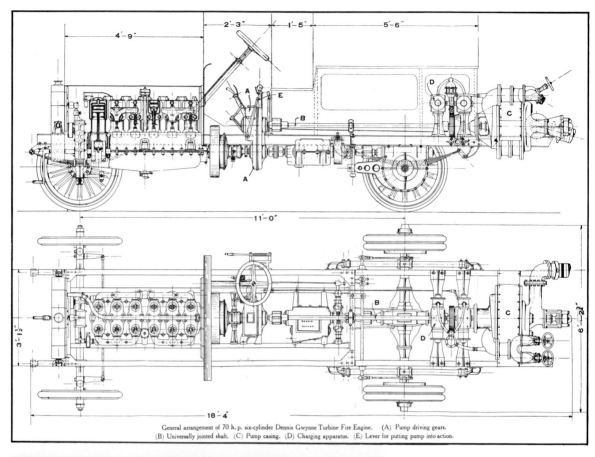

General arrangement of 70 h.p. six-cylinder Dennis Gwynne Turbine Fire Engine. (A) Pump driving gears.
(B) Universally jointed shaft. (C) Pump casing. (D) Charging apparatus. (E) Lever for putting pump into action.

Left This strange device of 1910 was a 'colonial' machine which combined the function of tractor, irrigation pump, crop sprayer and fire pump. The picture was taken on a test run with an 8-ton trailer before shipment to Australia.

Above By 1911 the fire engine had grown in stature with a 70 hp six-cylinder engine and over 600 gpm delivery from the pump.

Left Early postvans on the 30 cwt, 12 hp chassis of 1906 had stylish bodies to the specification of McNamara & Co who for many years carried the mails on contract for the GPO.

Above Fifty horsepower motor fire engines like this featured in countless controversies in papers like the *Yorkshire Post*, which championed the horse long after the motorised appliance had proved its superiority. This engine is seen outside the fire station in Keighley, West Yorks, in 1910.

Right A 40 hp chassis capable of carrying 2½-3 tons was available by the time of the Olympia Show in 1905. One of the first of these was sold to Hancock's Brewery in November that year, after being on the show stand.

A LOAD ON THEIR MINDS

Once the world became aware that Dennis Brothers were making commercial vehicles, things happened fast. The successes with the cars had not gone unheeded, and the reputation so gained led hard-headed commercial operators of buses, trucks and vans to listen carefully when new Dennis projects were mentioned. No sooner had the little van gone to work for its living than a bus chassis was produced, similar in broad concept but on a longer wheelbase, and with a 28 hp, four-cylinder Aster engine. The purchaser was one Benjamin Richardson, who planned a bus service between Kingston-on-Thames and Richmond, and who undertook to supply the bodywork himself. Imagine the disappointment of the Dennis brothers when this turned out to be a rather decrepit structure from an ancient horse bus! But the vehicle proved reliable and economical, and it was only a few weeks before the Mid-Sussex Motor Syndicate took delivery of the first of two new larger Dennises, both with new bodies.

The opportunity was taken to demonstrate the bus to the Press, representatives of which accompanied the first one to Sussex, and later spoke in glowing terms, notably of the smoothness and silence achieved by the transmission and the worm axle. There was considerable excitement a month or so later when an order for two buses came from Southend, where a new company had been set up to run them. During the eventual delivery trip to Southend, accompanied by vast numbers of associates and friends, they were alleged in contemporary reports to have called at most if not all of the hostelries along the way, taking 11 hours to cover about 40 miles, and were finally 'played in' at Southend by a brass band as dusk was falling.

Unfortunately the company had overlooked the detail of obtaining a licence to run the buses, so the celebration was short lived. That, however, was an exception and in that first year of bus production, machines went into successful service not only with many British fleets in major towns like London,

Cardiff, Birmingham and Manchester, but also in rural areas as far apart as Cornwall and Lincolnshire and overseas in Australia, New Zealand, Italy and Holland. Bus chassis with 28 or 35 hp were offered, all with the smooth-running worm axle and a patented freewheeling-layshaft gearbox.

Not satisfied with the successes of the bus business, the brothers Dennis turned their attentions not only to the development of heavy trucks, but to fire engines too. Up until that time in 1907, practically all the fire appliances in use were horse-drawn and the larger ones had steam pumps. It occurred to John Dennis that such an appliance would be able to reach a fire faster if it were motor powered, and the pumping operation would be vastly simpler, not to mention quicker to get going, if that too were motor powered. Calculations concerning the power required showed that something in the order of 50-60 hp would be needed, and that was rather more than any of the Aster engines provided.

They approached the Coventry engine manufacturers, White and Poppe Ltd, who agreed to supply the appropriate engines, and work commenced on designing a motor fire appliance. It was a splendidly simple and practical machine, with a conventional front-engined chassis layout and, of course, the worm drive, a four-speed gearbox similar to the bus chassis, and a power take-off above the transmission to drive a rear-mounted pump. A Gwynne turbine pump was chosen, as it seemed to John that such a device must have considerably less internal friction than a piston pump, and also be less sensitive to dirt in the water it was pumping. However, his opinion was by no means universally accepted, and for many years after that date, controversy raged between the respective merits of the two types of pump. Dennis engines always had turbine pumps, however, initially supplied by Gwynne Pumps and later made in Dennis's own workshops.

That first Dennis motor fire engine went to the

City of Bradford Fire Brigade in the spring of 1908, and was an immediate success. Fire chiefs from all over Britain went to Bradford to see the machine, and most went to Guildford shortly afterwards to order one for themselves. London Fire Brigade did not get their first motor engine until 1910, but thereafter became the largest single customer for Dennis engines. The production facility at Onslow Street rapidly became inadequate, and further premises were sought, not to replace the main works but to supplement them.

The solution came from a most unlikely source. A church mission hall in Brixton, south London, was advertised for sale in 1908, and as it was a sectional building of very large dimensions, Raymond went to look at it and bought it. It was transported down to Guildford piece by piece, and built up on a site which was (in those days) just outside the town at a place called Woodbridge. That is where the current Dennis headquarters is located, of course, and has been for many years. But then it was a piece of spare ground, so it was levelled and the old mission hall erected on it, complete with wooden floors. A large sign on the outside proclaimed that this was the works where Dennis fire engines and buses were made. Its 29,000 sq ft of floorspace were carefully organised to accommodate the bodybuilding and forging activities, as well as the assembly of the larger chassis. There was a canteen too, an indication of the company's attitude to labour relations. At that time such facilities were unusual. That building is still there among the much larger sprawl of today's Woodbridge works, known simply as No 1 shop.

The effects of that second-hand building were dramatic. The vast increase in working space permitted an immediate expansion in heavy vehicle production, and one of the big problems at Onslow Street, which had been built primarily with cars in mind, was that it would only accommodate limited numbers of commercials which might be well over 20 feet long, the bodies for which were built separately, so doubling the floorspace occupied. As with many companies, there was a 'chicken or egg' decision to make; wait for a demand then build it, or create the production capacity and hope it would be needed. Dennis had chosen the former course, and went out to create the demand for their vehicles by every possible means.

One of the most important of those means was the commercial vehicle trial. These were very popular in the early part of the century, having developed from the steam wagon trials of the late 1890s. All kinds of organisations ran commercial trials, ranging from local chambers of commerce to the trade Press, the object being to see which vehicles stood up best to hard work and performance tests.

The nearest thing to those trials we see these days are private trials run by individual fleet buyers, and the group tests of batches of six or seven trucks run by the more enterprising trade journals, like *Truck* magazine's European Supertest series. The trouble in 1907 was that there were too many trials and the results were too fragmented to be of much general use.

Consequently the industry approached the Royal Automobile Club, which at that time was as deeply involved with commercial vehicles as it was with passenger cars. They arranged a trial which was to start in London, with all the entries carefully checked to make sure they were representative machines, not built specially for the trial. They would then spend several weeks driving with varying loads all over Britain, while speeds, consumptions, breakdowns, repairs, parts used, time keeping, hill climbing, traffic behaviour, load protection, brake performance, handling and many other items were carefully recorded by observers travelling on the vehicles.

There were 60 entries in that great trial in the late summer of 1907, of which only three were steam driven, the remainder being divided into seven weight classes of 10 cwt, 1 ton, 30 cwt, 2 tons, 3 tons, 5 tons and 6 tons and over, all these being carrying capacity. Dennis entered vehicles in the 30 cwt, 2-ton, 3-ton and 5-ton classes, all borrowed from fleets of users of Dennis trucks. This was not only good advertising for the firms concerned, like Harrods Stores and Maples the furnishers, but it presented a more convincing picture to the effect that they were production vehicles and not trials specials. It also meant that any teething or settling-down troubles would be behind them. The day-by-day fortunes or otherwise of the contestants were widely reported in the national, regional and trade Press, with almost as much public interest as a major motor rally might enjoy today.

After more than a month, of which 22 days were fully occupied by driving, all the Dennis entries finished the course. The 2-tonner won a silver medal in its class, second only to the much more experienced manufacturer, Milnes Daimler, while the other three all received commendations in their respective classes. The prizes were not rich, but the dependable progress of the four Dennis trucks throughout the trial did not go unnoticed in industry. A firm that could build successful trucks in all sizes, they argued, must have something in its favour.

The fully detailed results of the trials were not finally published until well into 1908, but enough was made known before then to mean a steady increase in the number of enquiries at Guildford.

Consequently when the mission hall was erected at Woodbridge, its capacity was already urgently required to fulfil a backlog of orders. Generally speaking the larger chassis were built at Woodbridge along with the buses and fire engines, while smaller ones, especially the 30 cwt and 2-tonners were built alongside the cars at Onslow Street.

That pattern of work continued through to the end of the decade, with an enormous number of variants of the basic chassis built to customers' special requirements. The versatility in the Dennis chassis was its great virtue. Not only could one component be adapted to work equally well on several chassis versions, so reducing the manufacturing cost, but 'special' chassis could be supplied at very little more than the price of a standard vehicle. By the time the rumblings of war began in 1912-13, and a re-organisation took place within Dennis, heavy vehicle production was in the region of 300 a year, of which about one fifth were fire engines.

A restructuring of the company was called for due to its rapid expansion, and the need for wider sources of capital, which were very quickly forthcoming when the shares of the new Dennis Brothers (1913) Ltd were offered on the market. But to the common man, there were more important things than share dealings to think about. It was quite clear that Europe was heading for a war. As early as 1911, the War Office department of the UK Government made it clear that they were interested in having a large pool of reliable motor vehicles that they could mobilise quickly in the event of war breaking out.

In due course they developed their 'subvention' scheme often, but incorrectly, called the subsidy scheme, by which vehicles meeting with official approval after exhaustive tests could be bought by private transporters on the understanding that they would be handed over to the War Office immediately on demand in time of war. Advantages were to be found on both sides. The user received a payment each year he had the vehicle, assuming that it was kept in good condition, and the army had an immediate supply of vehicles. Furthermore, both parties were assured of a good truck, because the development trials for the subvention scheme were extremely severe, and a lot of work had to be done before even the excellent Dennis vehicles could meet the laid down requirements.

The initial trucks submitted for test were 3-tonners with Aster engines, and apart from some detail points on chassis fittings and maintenance, they did fairly well. There was, however, one major proviso inserted in the report by the War Office engineers. They wanted more flexibility in the engine, and greater ability to work flat out for a longer period, without water temperature approaching boiling. It was at this point that the White and Poppe engine finally became the standard fitment on all Dennises, although it had been used in the heavier chassis for some time. The radiator was also modified at that time to a very robust cast-frame type with finned replaceable tubes forming the cooling matrix. The evolution of that subvention 3-tonner marked a change in appearance too. Gone were the old spindly spring brackets, the sheet metal radiator tanks and the wooden wheels. In their place were modern, tough components, and they were to remain largely unchanged for nearly 15 years.

Including both civilian machines mobilised under the subvention scheme and those built specifically for the War Office during the period of hostilities from 1914-18, over 7,000 of those tough 3-tonners went to war. Plans were made to supply Allied armies too—evidenced by submission drawings in French and Flemish, but no record exists that any such contracts materialised. Dennis were not alone in the subvention system, of course. Leyland and Thornycroft featured largely in the scene, along with some smaller makers. From a practical point of view it was an excellent scheme, and the durability and numbers of all those trucks made sure that the forces fighting in Europe never lacked mobility.

The rapid build-up to the production required as a result of the subvention participation, meant extra facilities at Woodbridge. Three additional large workshop buildings were completed in less than two years all coming into full use during 1911-12, and by 1916 three further shops were added, while some of the older ones were extended. Together with the new office block completed in 1916 (which still forms Dennis headquarters today) the covered factory area was almost 300,000 sq ft or 33,000 sq m, which made it one of the largest commercial vehicle factories in Europe at the time. To power that plant, a self-contained generating station was built, using Sulzer diesels, and that installation still provides independent power for the factory.

In the meantime, things had not been entirely uneventful on the less war-like front of the fire engine and the motor bus. Development of passenger vehicles proceeded quickly after the basic technical needs of those early models had been mastered. Lower frames, softer springs, cushion tyres as an interim between solids and pneumatics, greater carrying capacities, better performance, all received attention. Thus, by the time war broke out, you could have a Dennis in either single- or double-deck form that carried twice the passengers at higher speed on less fuel than the Mid-Sussex Motor Syndicate could, just a few short years before. Practically every fire brigade in the country, and literally hundreds more overseas, learned the virtues of the Dennis engine, although that path was not without its obstructions.

A Dennis engine got stuck in a mixture of mud, ice and snow trying to get round the back of a burning wool mill in Bradford, and the mill rapidly burned out during the 45 minutes needed to extricate the heavy machine. The *Yorkshire Post* ran a major article about the inefficiency of motor fire engines, and said the disaster could have been averted by using horses. That was on January 1 1914, but one suspects that it was a last desperate call by a horse-enthusiast editor, for on the very same day *The Times* reminded its readers that no city or town should be without its motor fire engine, 'which is infinitely superior in speed, power, and its sheer ability to quench large conflagrations'. *The Times*, not given to free advertising, even went so far as to mention that, 'special enterprise has been shown in this direction by Messrs Dennis Brothers of Guildford'. Bradford finally pensioned off its remaining horses six weeks after the mill incident, to the accompaniment of disproportionately extensive news and picture coverage in the *Yorkshire Post*. The same week, London's last fire horses were put out to graze. The motor engine had won the day, inevitably in hindsight, and despite the cost of well over £1,000 for a standard 50 hp appliance, municipalities queued at the Dennis door to place their orders.

Just how closely aligned to fire prevention Dennis had become despite the huge output of trucks and buses, was illustrated by a report in the trade Press about the Great Northern Motor Show, held in Manchester City Hall in February 1914. It seemed, according to at least two reports, that the Dennis exhibit — a fire engine — was opposite the Daimler stand containing a large truck with a huge load of cotton bales, a material prone to spontaneous combustion if stacked for too long. The Dennis men spent the show hoping and praying that the cotton would do just that so that they could go and extinguish it. Needless to say, their services were not required.

However, there were real fires to deal with, literally and figuratively speaking, in the years that followed. Over 7,000 people worked at Dennis and the factory continued 24 hours a day non-stop for four years. That taught many new lessons in production, while the demands of military specifications taught further lessons in material and quality control. When the long dreary conflict finally ground to a halt, and weary Britons celebrated the event in battlefield, workshop and city squares, Dennis found itself a great deal larger and stronger than it had at the outbreak of that war. In the event, success in the peace-time contest was scarcely less arduous than the war had been. But this time it was a different kind of enemy, an economic enemy, and many would be the casualties. Immediately the armistice was signed, the Dennis board met to plan their future critical years.

The two infamous Southend buses, which amid great revelry at many hostelries, made a slow delivery trip late in 1907 only to find that public service was impossible as the proprietors had neglected to obtain the necessary licences.

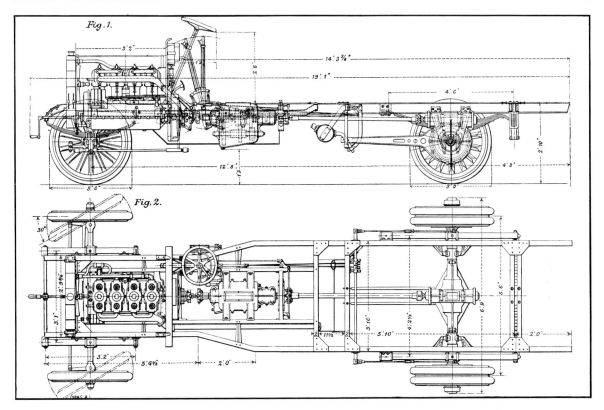

Fig.1.

Fig.2.

Above left The first of two buses sold to Mid-Sussex Motor Syndicate sets off on a Press demonstration from Guildford on July 13 1905. There appear to be 14 passengers outside and only two inside.

Above The new bus chassis which appeared in 1907 embodied many advanced features including a very sturdy gearbox with a freewheeling layshaft. This chassis was developed as a 3-ton truck in 1908.

Left In 1908 the motor cab was more popular than it was reliable, consequently Dennis developed a special recovery truck with a winch for bringing 'dead' cabs back to their depots. Two of the biggest operators, Gamage-Bell, and General Motor Cab Co, were the first to use them.

Right Typical Dennis chassis construction depicted in a 40 hp chassis. The gearbox is mounted remotely from the engine, both are mounted on a subframe, semi-flexibly attached to the main chassis. This model has an open propeller shaft.

Left and below left Dennis 3-ton tippers were popular with local authorities before World War 1 for tasks like road maintenance and repair of banks and dykes.

Below Special sidings were put in at Guildford for the purposes of delivering the vast numbers of fire engines built from 1908 onwards. This pair would go by rail to Liverpool, then one would go on board a ship bound for Australia.

Right Scores of ambulances like this were supplied to the London Asylums Board before 1910. They marked the start of a long line of Dennis ambulances.

Below right A 12-seater 'colonial' charabanc built for Australia, pictured before shipment in 1908. The tyres are the KT block type designed to give a soft ride as well as good grip on the road.

The above Mail Vans are——
DENNIS CARS.

They run with Reliability, Regularity and Economy.

That is why

Messrs. McNamara and Co. have 23 Dennis Cars.
Metropolitan Asylums Board have 18 Dennis Cars.
Harrods, Ltd., have 17 Dennis Cars.
Carter Paterson and Co. have 9 Dennis Cars.
Maple and Co. have 8 Dennis Cars.
Lever Bros. have 6 Dennis Cars.

THESE REPEAT ORDERS SPEAK VOLUMES.

WRITE FOR PARTICULARS TO—
DENNIS BROS., LIMITED, GUILDFORD.

DENNIS'S A.B.C.

Not only users BUT ACTUAL PURCHASERS

N.B.—Space obviously precludes us putting in more than a FEW purchasers.

A. AERATED WATER MANUFACTURERS.
Direct Supply Co., Kingston.

B. BISCUIT MFRS.
Peek, Frean and Co., London.
McFarlane, Lang & Co., London.

BREWERS.
Whitbread and Co., London.
Gateside Brewers, Newcastle.
Hancock and Co., Cardiff.
Fremlin Bros., Maidstone.
Arnold, Perrett, Gloucester.

C. CAB COMPANIES.
General Motor Cab Co., London.
Oxford Motor Cab Co.
Antonio Dantas, Lisbon.
T. W. Osgood, Sydney, Australia.

COCOA MFRS.
Cadbury Bros., Bourneville.

CO-OPERATIVE SOCIETIES.
Barnsley British Co-op.
Bradford Co-op.
Brighouse Co-op.
Derby Co-op.

COAL COMPANIES.
Bengal Coal Co.
Drake and Mount, Camberley.

CORPORATIONS
(Fire Engines, etc.)
Birkenhead.
Bradford.
Glasgow.
Kingston.
Oldhull (Static).

D. DRAPERS.
Wm. Laird Bros., London.
Grant and Co., Croydon.
Dewhirst and Spinks, Leeds.

DRUGGISTS.
May and Sons, London.
Willows, Francis, Butler and Thomson Ltd., London.

DYERS.
Ripley Dye Works.
Bradford Dyers' Association.

E. ENGINEERS.
Sturdy Engineering Co., Singapore.
Fras. Greenwood, Leeds.
Sir W. G. Armstrong, Whitworth and Co., Newcastle.
Adair Engineering Co., London.

F. FURNITURE.
Harrod's Stores, London.
Maple and Co., London.
Wm. Whiteley, Ltd., London.

G. GAS COMPANIES.
Gas Light and Coke Co., London.
South Metropolitan Gas Co.

GARAGES.
Thos. Dyson, Ltd., Bradford.
Bracewell, Hereford.
Mann, Egerton, Norwich.
McIntosh, Sydney.
Rossleigh, Ltd., Edinburgh.
Rennie and Prosser, Glasgow.
Sully's Ltd., Cardiff.

GOVERNMENTS.
Crown Agents for the Colonies.

H. HOTEL PROPRIETORS.
J. Ranson, Esq., Guildford.
T. Lloyd, Esq., Cardigan.
H. Clarke, Esq., Farnham.
B. Chandler, Esq., Hindhead.

I. ICE MERCHANTS.
Edwin Clarke and Co., Aldershot.

J. JOB MASTERS.
M. Puttock and Son, Guildford.
Mr. Crouch, Stoughton.
Mr. Sargood, Buryfields.
Thos. Tilling, Ltd., London.

K. KARRIERS (!)
McNamara and Co., Ltd., London.
Coburn Motor Co., Kent.
Carter, Paterson and Co., London.
Pickford and Co., Brighton.
Rio de Janeiro Carrying Co.

L. LAUNDRIES.
Filton Laundry, Bristol.
Horns Laundry, Kent.

M. MAIL SERVICES.
Mail Motor Co., Grimsby.
McNamara and Co., Ltd., London.
M. Puttock and Son, Guildford.
Wright, Dereham.
L. F. Mathews, Bishop Stortford.

N. NEWS VENDORS and PUBLISHERS.
W. H. Smith and Sons, London.
Bradbury, Agnew and Co., London.

NURSERYMEN.
Luxford, Covent Garden.

O. OMNIBUS PROPRIETORS.
Thos. Tilling, Ltd., London.
Gt. Eastern Omnibus Co., London.
Provincial Motor Tramways, Cardiff.
Gt. Grimsby Tramways Co.
Automobile Co., N.Z.
W. J. Randall, Andover.

P. PETROL IMPORTERS.
P.G.R. Co., Newcastle.

PASSENGER VEHICLES (Char-a-bancs).
Llandudno Motor Co.
A. C. Jones, Musselburgh.
Adam Young, Dalkeith.
Dr. Vivers, Sydney.
T. W. Osgood, Sydney.
Spencer, Southend.
Lloyd, Cardigan.
Booker, Barnsley.
E. W. Jackson, Doncaster.
F. Caffrey, Doncaster.
J. Risk, Huddersfield.
C. G. Steadman, Doncaster.

PUBLIC BOARDS.
Metropolitan Asylums Board, London
West Ham Union.

PROVISION DEALERS.
Gurney and Co., Hereford.
H. Shanks, Surrey.

Q. QUICK SERVICE TRANSPORT.
Coburn Motor Co., Kent.
Central Transport Co., London.
McNamara and Co., London.

R. REPOSITORIES.
Wm. Whiteley, Ltd., London.
Maple and Co., London.
Harrods Stores, London.

S. SOAP MFRS.
Lever Bros., Port Sunlight.

T. TOBACCO MFRS.
Imperial Tobacco Co.

TRAVELLERS' BUSES.
W. Watts, Manchester.

U. UPHOLSTERERS, Etc.
Maple and Co., London.

V. VARNISH MFRS.
Aldridge, Islington.

W. WAGON BUILDERS.
Bristol Wagon and Carriage Co.
Healey and Sons, Gloucester.
Storeys, Ltd., Nottingham.

X. 'XPORTERS.
Lazer, Kemsley and Fisher, London.
Jacob Walton and Co., London.
Dick Kerr and Co., London.

Be a Y. Z. (Wise head !) AND
Write at once for our New Catalogue.

DENNIS BROS., LTD., GUILDFORD.

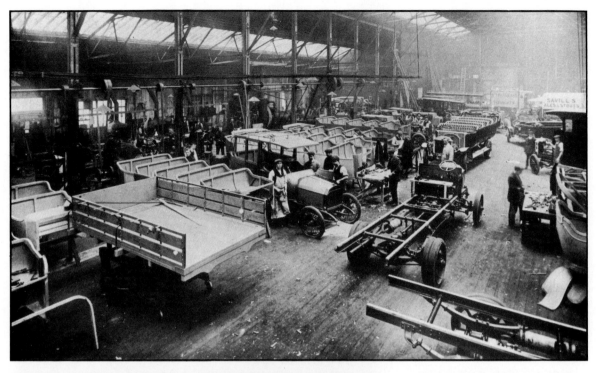

Previous two pages Dennis Brothers believed in powerful advertising. This is just one of many used in the period from 1909 up to World War 1.

Above The new works at Woodbridge in 1910 was busily turning out cars, trucks, charabancs, vans and taxicabs, all in one splendidly confused assembly area.

Left In the years before World War 1, part-time soldiering was considered great fun and few foresaw the seriousness of the forthcoming conflict. But in the meantime, crowds turned out to watch the young men on their manoeuvres. Here the County of London Territorial regiment overloads a hired 25 cwt Dennis in 1909.

Above right All set for a great day out: 28 excited voyagers gather aboard a 35 hp charabanc operated by Puttock s the Guildford motor agents. The year was 1911.

Right Some of the new Dennis vans in McNamara's fleet ready to set off from Mount Pleasant sorting office in London. These big vans took the mails to distant cities like Southampton and Norwich.

Background photograph Part of an order of more than 70 Dennis vans delivered to McNamara's to carry the Royal Mails, lines up for delivery at Woodbridge in July 1912. Overnight all London's horsedrawn mails were replaced by motor vans.

Inset By the end of the first decade of the century Dennis buses were a common sight. The Great Western Railway — long a good Dennis customer — used buses like this 20-seater to feed their railheads. This bus ran from Truro round the Lizard and was photographed at Porthleven in 1911.

Above Typical of the type of customer attracted by the reliability of Dennis trucks were the nation's merchants and traders. This 2½-tonner was one of a Dennis fleet used by Leigh (Lancs) Co-operative Society. The picture was taken in 1911.

Left At the outbreak of war, experiments were made at Guildford in running vehicles on town-gas, contained in a huge bag on the roof. The truck here is a well-worn 2-tonner of about 1910.

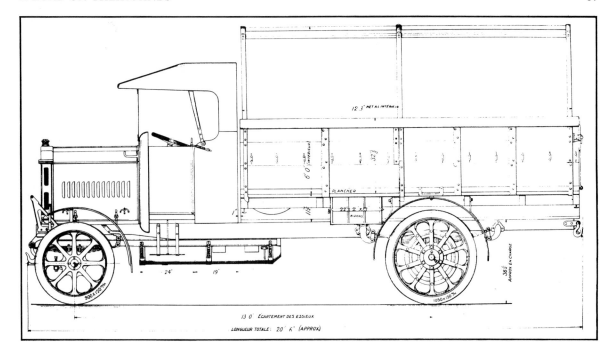

Above The 3-ton subvention model developed under War Office auspices was built in large numbers. As this drawing with French annotations shows, the subvention scheme was intended to serve all the Allied nations, but few served in other than the British forces. This drawing is dated 1913.

Four stages in the saga of the 3-ton War Office subvention truck. **Above right** An early trials model. **Title page** Taking part in the trials run by the War Office with Leyland, Hallford Maudslay and Commer behind. **Right** Volume-produced trucks going off to the Western Front. **Overleaf top** Victorious 'Tommies' in a newly liberated Rouen with their Dennis in 1918.

Below Early trailer pumps were made during World War 1, both for fire fighting and drinking water supply. In the two wars and the period between them, more than 11,000 trailer pumps were made.

THE GOLDEN YEARS AT GUILDFORD

That first board meeting after the armistice in 1918 was perhaps the most important in the company's history. The intensive war effort had expanded their company immensely, bringing them vast production capacity and new skills. What to do with all that now, faced with uncertain trade climates, gloomy economic forecasts, and no all-embracing incentive? Nicholas Andrew was chairman at the time, and the Dennis brothers were joint managing directors. Reggie Downing, the fire engine chief, was also on the board. With their colleagues they decided on a two-pronged attack on the new world in front of them. On the one hand they would diversify their activities into other engineering fields, and secondly they would intensify their export activity.

Raymond Dennis set off on a 60,000-mile world tour to study conditions, and assess users' demands. He had plenty to offer potential customers. He could, for example, point to the magnificent record of the 3-tonners in dreadful conditions on the war fronts. He could remind municipalities that a pair of Dennis fire engines had pumped dirty harbour water non-stop for over a week during the great Salonika fire in 1917. He could point to the diversity and durability of the product. But most of all he could promise quick delivery because Dennis had huge production capacity—something like 1,800 vehicles a year if need be, and in 1919 that was big production in the truck field. While he was away Raymond learned that he was to be invested with the Knight Bachelor order, so henceforth he would be known as Sir Raymond. It seemed hard on his brother that he received no award for the company's efforts during the war, for they always worked as a close team, but the distinction never worried either of them.

While Raymond was assessing the world's needs, his fellow directors at home were equally busy. New trucks were introduced, together with very advanced buses, all at unbelievably low prices, and work was assured for the factory. Dennis needed all the engines that White and Poppe could build, and in 1919 that company was absorbed into Dennis, Alfred White and Peter Poppe joining the Dennis board where they continued to be responsible for engines for many years. Plans were laid for diversification into other fields such as mowing machines, industrial pump sets, and municipal appliances. By that time, the company offices had all been moved to Woodbridge, and the firm took the simple title of Dennis Brothers Ltd. It all looked rosy enough, but clouds were already gathering. The first taste of industrial unrest came with the foundry moulders' strike of 1919, which only partially affected Dennis, but showed what the next few years might have in store.

Inevitably perhaps, turnover, production and profits dropped slightly after the frantic war years, though not disastrously so, as it had done in some less prudent firms. But by 1922 business really began to take off, largely as a result of Raymond's close study of world needs, and with old dealers around the world revitalised, and a lot more new and enthusiastic outlets, production soared to an all-time high of almost 2,000 heavy chassis in 1923, and stayed at that level or slightly above until the world slump of the early 1930s.

Truck production revolved around improved versions of the 3-tonner which had seen Dennis through the war, and 4- and 5-tonners using similar techniques proved extremely popular too. Pneumatic tyres appeared, first on the smaller chassis, then on larger ones. The public in the 'roaring twenties' were insistent on enjoying themselves, and an impressive series of charabancs and, later, coaches emerged. Passenger services running to schedules over long distances grew rapidly, as did the popularity of the day or weekend trip to the seaside or the country in a 'chara'. All those model-series flourished, but still more was to come.

With the rapid growth in demand for housing, and the increasing population in those post-war years, municipal authorities were getting worried about the physical problems of street cleaning, rubbish collection, and the emptying and cleaning of drainage gullies and cesspools. It was a field of engineering a lot less glamorous than buses and fire engines, but no less essential. Thoughts at Guildford turned to the design of machines that would do these tasks mechanically, mounted of course on truck chassis, instead of the hand-methods and horses and carts universally employed up to that time, which were not without their perils to the neighbourhood when in action!

Dennis met the problem with a vacuum-emptying system which collected all the cesspool contents relatively harmlessly into a tank, which was then discharged again safely at the sewage farms. It was an immense improvement on older methods, not least in health aspects, and when the machine was first announced in 1921, local authorities flocked to investigate it. With refinements like a reversible pump that produced vacuum or air-pressure in the 750-gallon tank at will, and a range of fittings and features designed to handle almost any sewage or drainage problem, the new municipal vehicle department at Guildford got off to a flying start, and the vehicles sold literally in their hundreds. From those machines followed refuse vehicles, street washers and road sweeping machines. Roadsweepers were eventually discontinued, but the other types of local-authority vehicle have since that time remained a mainstay of Dennis activity.

As the 1920s ground uncertainly on, with neither industry nor government sure about economic or labour situations, the biggest Dennis yet appeared at the 1924 show. It was a 6-ton payload machine with either a 40 or 50 hp engine, and the improved four-speed Dennis gearbox. Its axle layout broke new ground, for instead of a horn type of torque reaction bracket to keep the drive axle located under full power, a torque tube anchored to a crossmember and bolted to the axle case, with the drive shaft down the centre, appeared for the first time. It was a remarkably sturdy truck, and certainly one of the best of its period. It was very light too at under 3½ tons tare, and with a price tag of £850 upwards, according to wheelbase, it was excellent value in comparison with steam wagons and other petrol trucks available in that capacity class.

That new design marked the beginning of a new era in Dennis truck design. Until then, there had been a marked similarity among all the chassis right through from around 1909, and only detail design had changed. From that point in the mid-1920s onwards, rapid advances were made, not only in vehicle and engine design, but in production economics and service support. That was a matter of

a positive attitude to the problems of the day, because already some firms were in trouble in a faltering market. At Dennis they felt their best chance of survival was to develop advanced, modern vehicles, and sell them at very competitive prices. That policy took them through the worst years of the Depression that was to follow, without ever failing to make a satisfactory trading profit. Very few motor manufacturers could claim such an achievement.

Meanwhile, despite the approaching gloom of the Depression — or perhaps because of it — the British public was intent on getting out and seeing the country, and enjoying itself in the process. A new passenger chassis with its cylinder block all in one piece appeared in 1925, with pneumatic tyres as an option to the cushion type, on which closed saloon type coachwork could be offered. It was one of these Dennises, in the fleet of the Greyhound Motor Co that began the first scheduled road carriage service between Bristol and London in 1925, pioneering what eventually became the world's finest road passenger service network, covering literally every town and city in Britain by the mid-1930s. Competing operators scheduled their services to link up with their neighbours, and traffic volumes soared. The first real competitor to rail travel in almost 90 years had at last arrived.

However, town bus operators were strangely reluctant to adopt pneumatic tyres, perhaps because of the mass of regulations which surrounded their use. It was one of the London independents, the 'Admiral' fleet which competed against the LGOC fleet, which first persuaded the authorities (which included Scotland Yard) to allow them to run stage carriage services on pneumatics and that took place in the summer of 1925.

Four-wheel brakes had an equally difficult path to acceptance, and it was only after prolonged demonstrations and campaigning, using the new E type Dennis bus, that they were finally permitted on public service buses in 1926.

Throughout that mid-1920s era, new model followed new model, each superior to its predecessor, and invariably lower in price too. The 6-tonner was the first 'new generation' chassis in 1924, followed by an exciting new 36 bhp, 30 cwt model in 1925 which, like the 6-tonner, had a new type of cylinder block cast all in one piece with the crankcase, and a clutch housing and gearbox all bolted together in a single unit. This was termed 'unit construction' in the industry, and although it was already familiar in light vehicles, notably the Morris 1-tonner that had succeeded in winning back a large proportion of the light truck market from import machines after its introduction in 1924, it was a new concept for heavier chassis. Dennis finally abandoned the sub-frame as a means of mounting their power trains, and instead mounted the engine/transmission assembly on three rubber-bushed mountings in the chassis. Fame came for Dennis yet again when the Royal Family ordered two new 30 cwt vans to fetch and carry the Royal goods and chattels between Buckingham Palace and Windsor Castle, gaining them the coveted Royal Warrant insignia.

As 1925 drew to a close, two more new chassis appeared, the E and F types for bus and coach work. These too had new L-head sidevalve engines, with monobloc layout, and gearbox assembled in unit. The axle was still the famous Dennis worm type, but with a big difference. Instead of the worm being at the top of the axle, it was at the bottom, or 'underslung'. That enabled the propeller shaft to be mounted about ten inches lower in the chassis, which in turn allowed a much lower body floor to the bus. With facility for the driver alongside the engine, the E type in particular immediately gained hundreds of orders for Dennis. Four-wheel servo brakes were fitted too, and it was this advanced machine which finally broke through the London bus regulations about two-wheel brakes only.

By the following year there was a new double-decker too, known as the HV, which followed most of the trends of the E type, but had vacuum brakes for the first time on a passenger vehicle. That HV model continued virtually unchanged until 1930, an indication of its sound design in the first instance. Yet another model appeared in 1927, which was a development of the already-famous 30 cwt. It had a dropped-level frame, longer, softer springs, four-wheel brakes, the underslung worm axle, pneumatic tyres twinned at the rear, and new, more precise cam and roller steering gear. It was known as the G type, an immediate success in a wide variety of uses. It made a splendid ambulance chassis, for example, and hundreds saw service as buses and coaches with about 20 seats. There were shooting brakes, livestock transporters and mobile shops too.

As the 1920s drew to a close, Dennis built their largest, heaviest chassis to date, the 12-ton six-wheeler. That chassis had tandem worm axles, a 100 bhp engine shared with the buses, and an imposing forward control cab. The model made rapid advances into areas which had been the preserve of Leyland and Thornycroft, and gained considerable public exposure when one was used to ship Kay Don's racing Sunbeam 'Silver Bullet' to the docks on its way to America for a record attempt. But by then the Depression was biting industry hard. Unemployment was soaring, few companies were buying new trucks, although there was still a lively bus business, and to make things worse there was a lot of politically inspired tinkering with road traffic regulations. The trend at Guildford went away from heavy trucks, and for a while concentrated on buses and municipal vehicles, and of course the lawn mowers which had developed into a successful sideline. Many notable estates used Dennis mowers, including Windsor Castle.

In 1930 the E type bus was superseded by the Arrow, and the HV by the Lance, both representing considerable evolution in the respective fields of single- and double-deck buses. The Lance steadily grew from then on, and 15 years later there was still a clear resemblance in many chassis features, so good was that original 1930 design. It had a lowered and offset propeller shaft to permit a very low floor, which in turn reduced overall height, and fully loaded it would tilt to 40° comfortably without danger of toppling over. Together with the Arrow, those early Lance chassis had a new Dennis six-cylinder engine, an ingenious overhead camshaft type, in which the whole top-end assembly could be swung up on the camshaft axis to give access to valves. That did away with the main drawback of ohc engines, that of access to valves for decarbonising and regrinding. The Arrow was an advanced machine, very comfortable and fast, and a fine vehicle for the expanding inter-city passenger routes which were fast developing. But it was expensive at well over £1,000, and to the Dennis board, it was no machine to tackle the problems of the Depression.

They had already decided that for the next few years bus and municipal vehicles would be the best bet, but in 1931 they shook the commercial vehicle world to its foundations, by showing a new bus chassis at the Olympia Exhibition at not much more than half the price of the splendid Arrow. It had a rather lumpy, big-bore, four-cylinder engine, a very simple chassis and four-speed gearbox, vacuum brakes, a new worm and nut steering gear, and a remarkably full inventory of chassis equipment. You could have all that for £598, a bargain indeed. The Guildford works had been geared up to produce them in quantity, and Depression or not, orders came flowing in. It was a master stroke of market strategy, a classic case of the right vehicle at the right time. By early 1932 the new Dennis, called the Lancet, was a familiar sight on the main bus routes, with coachwork by all the leading builders, including Weymanns, Harrington, Park Royal, and Brush. Dennis also bodied some chassis themselves.

That bold concept kept Dennis busy right through the Depression though limited numbers of other types provided a little variety in the shops. While other manufacturers found themselves in dire troubles, Dennis not only continued healthily in business, but never ceased to make a handsome profit. Compared with the huge profits and turnover of the early 1920s it was perhaps modest, but by any other standards it was more than satisfactory.

As the 1930s went by, and the aftermath of the Depression gradually receded, the time came for further adventurous thinking. A new Lancet, the Lancet II, was launched with longer wheelbase, more power from its petrol engine or alternatively the Dennis-Lanova pre-heat oil engine, which respectively gave 90 and 84 bhp. The speed range of the oiler was rather limited, so a five-speed, close-ratio gearbox was offered with it. But more important to customers who were rapidly getting used to renewed affluence were detail refinements in suspension, brakes and maintenance, as well as very luxurious bodywork. The price went up to just over £700 for the petrol chassis and £825 for the oiler. Unfortunately the Lanova system was never very popular, mainly because users demanded too much of it and tried to use it like a petrol engine. Dennis developed their own oil engine in 1934, a sturdy four-cylinder design called the 0-4. It had cylinder dimensions of 117 mm x 150 mm and developed a healthy 81 bhp at 1,800 rpm, with massive low speed torque. That engine's reliability and economy was legendary, and diesel Lancets brought new standards of economy to the bus and coach industry.

With Dennis's new five-speed overdrive gearbox, operators regularly recorded 17 mpg with over 30 passengers and their luggage. The secret of the engine was in its good breathing, with four valves per cylinder, augmented by mutli-hole injectors spraying into toroidal cavities in the piston crown. The concept is widely employed nowadays, but was quite unusual in 1934.

The success of that 0-4 and a companion petrol engine offered as an option in the Lancets, pointed the way back to modern truck production, and by 1937 a brand new model range under the collective name of 'Max' made its appearance, designed for 12 tons gross operation. That too was an immediate success, and the Max went on to become one of the best known Dennises ever. In the meantime there had been a considerable demand for a lighter truck of more modern concept than the G-derivatives that were still in production up to 1933. In due course the distinctive 40/54 cwt chassis appeared. The passenger version of it was called the Ace, but over the years the goods versions have also collected that label, although it is strictly speaking incorrect. These chassis had a set-back front axle, making them very manoeuvrable, and were built in every

conceivable commercial vehicle form—trucks, tractive units, fire engines, buses, coaches, municipal vehicles, mobile shops, rescue tenders, and anything else you can think of.

They sold in thousands overseas as well as in Britain, and two fire engines on this chassis were still in use in Barcelona just a year or two ago, and may still be. The fire engine and bus versions were particularly popular in rural districts because they could thread their way through country lanes very easily, with that set-back axle. For broadly similar reasons the railway companies and the breweries employed them in their thousands for use in narrow urban streets. A very fine specimen is preserved to this day in the livery of Shell Mex and BP Ltd, and can be seen on rallies occasionally, in the hands of an old friend of the author's, Brian Veale. There was a heavier version of the Ace, called, not illogically, the Mace, which in turn led to the development of a lighter companion to the Max immediately before war broke out, called the Pax. Its capacity was about 4½ tons in commercial terms, although subsequent military versions were very conservatively rated at a mere 3 tons while the 8-ton payload Max was labelled a 5-tonner.

As another war loomed darkly on the horizon, the Dennis factory was back to its old frantic activity of the early 1920s, indeed still more workshop space had been added so that over half a million square feet of covered space was available on the 31 acres of the site at Woodbridge. In the 1930s, Dennis had built a large number of houses for their employees, including a whole estate known as Dennisville, and they had set remarkably high standards for industrial housing. But with all that manufacturing space, and a closely knit community-workforce with high standards of skill and loyalty, it was a valuable asset to the nation in time of war.

No sooner had the declaration of hostilities been made in September 1939, than government officials began stepping off the London train in droves. A major change was imminent within the quiet and efficient corridors of Guildford. That change was not only due to the invasion from Whitehall, but something infinitely more important to the workforce. For just before the war officially broke out, both John and Raymond Dennis died, within a few weeks of each other. For the first time in almost half a century, there was no Mr John and no Mr Ray at the works. To many, that was a greater disaster than any war could have been.

The product of 28 years experience in the Motor manufacturing industry

MOTOR DENNIS MOWER

"I cannot speak too highly of the 'Dennis' as I consider it the best Motor Lawn Mower on the market."
Mr. C. H. Cook, Head Gardener, Royal Gardens, Windsor Castle.

"**The actual labour employed is now less than one-sixth**" (see p. 16)

Two men	11 hours
Horse and 2 men	7 hours
DENNIS MOTOR LAWN MOWER AND ONE MAN	3½ hours

DENNIS BROS. LTD.
GUILDFORD

'Phone: 575 Guildford (4 lines)   'Grams: Dennis, Guildford

Surrey County Cricket Clubs 'DENNIS' Mower at Work at Kennington Oval.

Above The mower catalogue of 1922 showed the effectiveness of the product but it also indicated that it was an expensive machine.

Right A Dennis mower prepares the sacred turf at Wembley stadium before a Cup Final.

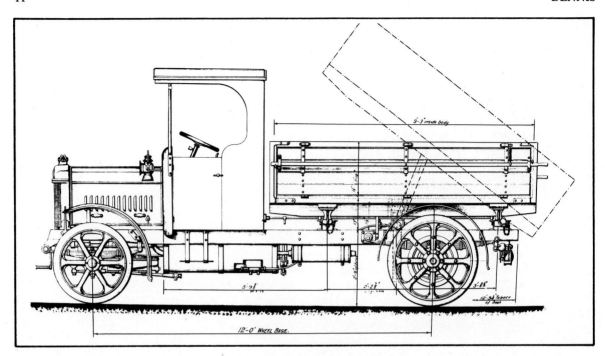

By 1919-20 the 2-tonner had grown much more sturdy and had a White and Poppe engine. Compare this drawing with the one of the 1907 chassis, particularly in items like spring brackets, frame dimensions, and wheel hubs.

For many years after the 3-ton subvention model was developed its design lived on. This drawing of the 1925 3-tonner shows many similarities with the 1913 chassis shown on page 37.

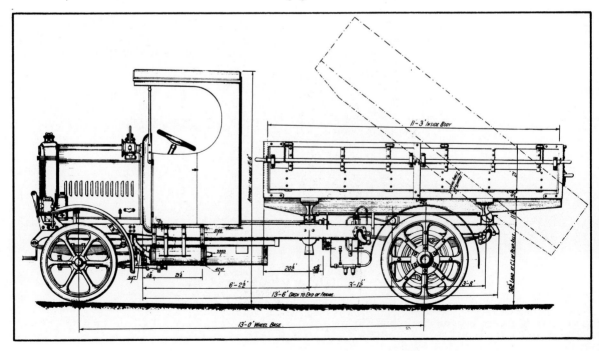

Above The early municipal vehicles of 1922 were primitive by modern standards, but they revolutionised the activities of local health authorities. Dennis has been a municipal vehicle specialist ever since.

Right The last T-head White and Poppe engines disappeared in 1925, giving way to monobloc L-head designs. By that stage the T-head engines had enclosed valves and pumped cooling water.

P.3

Facing page The new 30 cwt chassis introduced in 1925 was a thoroughly modern machine available in either bonnetted or forward control versions. They were extremely popular as parcels vans, and many big retailing chains used them as well as public carriers like these two.

Right A special long wheelbase version of the 30 cwt chassis was developed as a light fire appliance from 1926, and this relatively inexpensive machine proved popular at a time when local authority budgets were severely restricted.

Right The E type single-deck bus with its low-level transmission, four-wheel brakes and forward control, brought advanced engineering to the bus business in 1925.

Right The engine of the E type was the first Dennis unit to use the monoblock layout instead of cylinders cast in pairs.

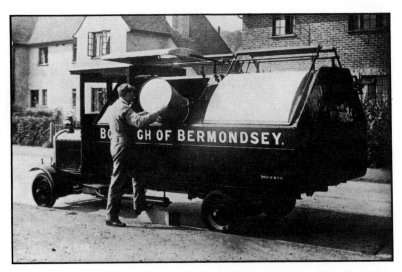

Left Special low-loading chassis for municipal work in the mid-1920s were based on 30 cwt chassis fitted with small diameter wheels. The low body made bin emptying much easier.

Below In 1927 an extremely modern and handsome ambulance was produced, based on the new G type of the 30 cwt chassis. Versions of this machine were built for ambulance corps all over Britain and many export markets too. There was also a bus/coach version.

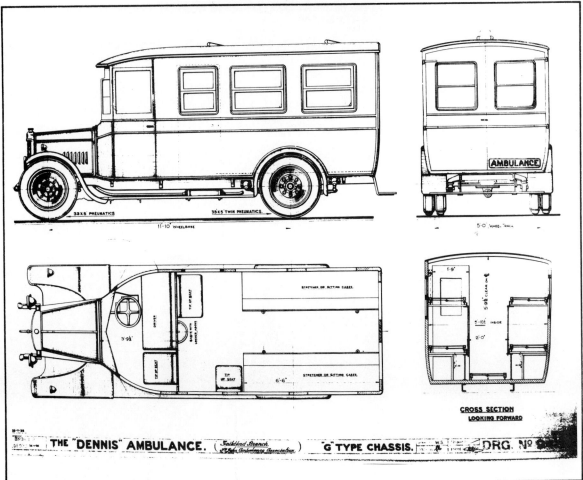

THE "DENNIS" AMBULANCE. (*Guildford Branch St John Ambulance Association.*)   'G' TYPE CHASSIS.   DRG. No

Right The 12-ton chassis took Dennis into the top weight class in 1929. It had a 100 hp engine and tandem worm drive axles.

Below The engine of the G type was one of the neatest designs ever to emerge from Guildford.

Background photograph Part of a massive order for Lance double-deckers, which were delivered to London in 1932. This is a 'trick' picture; the buses were delivered in twos and threes as they were completed. These groups were photographed at various points on the road outside the works, and finally all printed up together.

Inset An overhead camshaft engine developing just over 100 bhp was built from 1930 to 1936 for use in the Lance double-deck chassis and the 12-ton six-wheeler. Cylinder size was 110 mm x 140 mm and the whole valve and rocker group hinged round the camshaft axis to aid maintenance accessibility.

Left A Lance double-decker under-goes its statutory tilt test at the factory. The year is 1934. The tilt angle is 39° with the top deck fully loaded.

Below The Lanova was a pre-heat indirect injection oil engine, used in the early 1930s which developed 82 bhp. It was quickly superseded by Dennis's own direct injection engine.

Right Early Lancet bus chassis had a big four-cylinder petrol engine which gave a very satisfactory performance. Its popularity was enhanced by a chassis price of a mere £600—a bargain even in 1932. A few early Lancets had the 100 hp ohc engine.

Below right Lancet II single-deck chassis (left) and Lance double-deckers in the assembly shop in 1933.

The Falcon was a lightweight bus built for routes with weak bridge restrictions. The Southdown Motor Services Falcons worked on the route to Hayling Island. **Below** A Gardner 3.8-litre 4LK engine in a Falcon. Most Falcons had a 75 hp Dennis engine.

Above Special fire appliances for use in large cities were produced during the mid-1930s. They carried up to 15 firemen with their personal gear, plus minimal hose and pump equipment. Leeds, Birmingham and Manchester were among the principal users.

Right The 1935 Lancet II was more expensive than its predecessor but boasted more refinement. It was the first Dennis available with an oil engine, initially the Lanova type, and subsequently the four-cylinder Dennis 0 type. This is a Harrington bodied prototype.

Right Special coachwork by Burlingham on an Ace chassis gave an appropriate image to ground transportation at Liverpool's Speke airport in 1937.

Left Among numerous specialist municipal vehicles built in the mid-1930s was a narrow-cab version of the 40/45 cwt chassis for street washing.

Below The 0-6 Dennis diesel engine was fitted to later series Lance and Lancet passenger chassis and in numerous heavy goods models too. The early 0-6 was a 7.6 litre, 110 bhp engine, later enlarged to 8 litres and 120 bhp. The auxiliary drives are from the rear of the engine.

Dennis 40/45 cwt chassis, often incorrectly called Aces, were very popular with own-account users in the mid-1930s. These pictures show a tractive unit on parcels work with the London Midland and Scottish railway, a forward control version carrying handcarts for sliced bread delivery, and another tractive unit working on distribution with Fremlins brewery.

TROUBLE AND STRIFE

The 1939-45 war was no easy time for any company. It meant drastic changes in work patterns and products. It meant training new and unskilled hands as the regular men went away to fight. It meant strange working hours and stranger devices on the shop floor. But as with most firms in Britain, the task was tackled at Dennis with enthusiasm and good humour, and at the end of the day the job was well done.

Those men from the ministry who took the Southern Railway from Waterloo to Guildford had all kinds of plans in their briefcases. No, Dennis could not continue to build ordinary trucks and buses, and yes, they would build weapons of war. And that great factory must be camouflaged immediately. In reality the job of making such a big plant, outlined on two sides by railway lines and by a dual-carriageway bypass on the third, invisible from the air, was impossible. Nevertheless camouflage was applied, and it made the individual shops less easy to distinguish at least.

Major reorgnisation took place, perhaps to the greatest extent in the main assembly shop which was turned over to the assembly of Churchill tanks. Hulls, engines and transmissions were brought in from other manufacturers, and the Churchills were put together and tested, ready for shipment to the front, after gun testing at a military range. The rumble and clatter of those 35-ton machines was as familiar in Guildford as it was subsequently at El Alamein and Caen. Over 700 were turned out in four years, but that was only a relatively small part of the work. The War Office ordered 3,000 Max heavy trucks, 1,500 Pax 3-tonners, as well as several hundred 'Signals' bodies for mounting on Ford and Bedford chassis. Then there were 3,000 Lloyd carriers (a light-infantry armoured vehicle), and countless thousands of complete medium-weight bombs and fin-and-case assemblies for heavy bombs. There were also 7,000 trailer pumps for fire fighting purposes.

In between, the factory managed to turn out a few hundred municipal vehicles for use on UK military bases and in those few cities where a good enough case for a new purchase could be proved. There were very limited numbers of trucks for civilian use, mainly for hauliers with contracts to move military hardware from one factory to another in that giant production process which was collectively known as 'the war effort'.

In 1939, streamlined production methods had meant that around 1,500 people worked at Dennis. By 1940-41 that had more than doubled, much of the new workforce recruited from the families—the wives, sisters and girlfriends—of the men who had worked there for years but were now fighting a distant war. Despite the lack of engineering background and basic skills, the quality of their work was remarkable, and very few items were rejected by the ministry inspectors who checked everything before dispatch.

Later in the war Dennis built transmission units for Cromwell, Centaur and Comet tanks, and shipped them to what had been the rival factories of Foden and Leyland for installation in the complete vehicle. Such was the demand for all these diverse products that the factory worked 24 hours a day, seven days a week, and those on the off-duty shift took it in turns to watch the skies for air raids by day and night. Strangely enough the works was never attacked—maybe that camouflage did work after all—although some bombs fell in and around the town of Guildford itself, with little damage.

The Max in particular gained a first class reputation for itself throughout the war, in North Africa, Greece, Italy and the European campaigns. Indeed many of them served right through the war and were kept on in the peacetime army until well into the 1950s, so durable were they with their Dennis 'big four' engines. But the war ground to a halt, as had the previous one and, as the cost was counted, the feeling of anti-climax grew, and plans for the future were discussed. Once again it seemed that there would be no Utopian world for the returned warriors, although the post-war Socialist government laid plans for an ambitious welfare state. But there could be no welfare without industry, and industry must be nationalised, proclaimed the politicians. Along with the railways and the mines, road transport was in due course nationalised, and that meant a severe cut back in the truck output potential that had been planned, indeed already engineered at Dennis.

Spectacularly strong and economical trucks like the Jubilant and Max Major, as well as civilian versions of the Max and Pax, never got the chance to be used in quantity in hire-and-reward haulage. The state-owned transport fleet, British Road Services, tended to buy from just a few manufacturers like Leyland, AEC and Bedford, and largely ignored the rest, which was a short sighted policy, bad for the industry as a whole. Fortunately at Dennis it was not as disastrous as it might have been, because there was adequate potential in fire appliances, municipals, buses and ambulances. Other firms were not so fortunate, and that BRS policy spelled the end of some like Vulcan and Sentinel, while others were sorely damaged as a result. Meanwhile Dennis developed a new engine called the 0-6, which used a lot of the technology of the 0-4, but had smaller cylinders measuring 105 mm x 146 mm. It developed 110 bhp at 2,000 rpm, and was a very smooth and economical engine. So although the truck market was decidedly bleak in 1947 and for several years afterwards, the bus trade boomed, thanks to a public tired of restriction and austerity who demanded transport to the seaside and countryside which they had not seen for five years.

New Lancet models were built with the six-cylinder engines, distinguishable from the earlier ones by a long elegant radiator cast in aluminium. With the quiet and powerful easy-revving 0-6 engine and a new 0 type five-speed gearbox, the post-war Lancets were in big demand as long distance coaches. Similarly equipped Lance double-deckers were built in quantity too, and those bus and coach models could be found all over Britain and in many export markets as well.

New truck models like the Horla and Hefty were developed, but good though they were, they never reached anything like the production volume of the bus chassis. Indeed the only truck which reached anything that could be called volume production during that period was the Pax, a light chassis available in both normal and forward control versions, with an ohv, four-cylinder 80 bhp petrol engine developed from the pre-war series. This was very popular with breweries and own-account users,

who were outside the scope of nationalisation, even though their radius of operation was severely restricted.

New fire engines were in demand too, as many had been destroyed or simply worn out during the war years. A new lineage was commenced in 1946 with the F series, and the early F1 and F2 models were eagerly snapped up by brigades such as London which had suffered heavy losses. In rapid succession, change and improvement produced further versions, until the pattern settled down with the stylish and compact F7. That appliance with its derivatives saw Dennis and its customers through the next dozen years with splendid results. Many fire officers still reckon those F7s were the best machines they ever had.

However, the outside world marched on. Big companies like Leyland, AEC and Foden, strengthened by BRS orders, became very competitive in the market. Leyland in particular with a busy factory fought the bus markets very hard, and built trucks in vast quantities. AEC, having collected both Maudslay and Crossley as subsidiaries did likewise, while the Bristol group, also having been favoured by BRS, was very competitive in the bus field, having discontinued trucks.

Such competition was getting tough on the smaller independents like Dennis, and they had not grown as quickly as some groups. Good though their products were, the competition got steadily tougher. Leyland's PD2 and PD3 double-deckers, for example, were first class machines and keenly priced, as were the Royal Tiger underfloor-engined chassis of the early 1950s. Dennis countered with an underfloor-engined Lancet for both bus and coach work, and a new double-decker chassis called the Loline. The new chassis enjoyed a considerable degree of success, and fleets in the north of England ran them for several years, as well as the more Dennis-orientated operators in the home counties. But the flat-engined single-deckers were less successful, prone to cooling problems and frame fractures, and they soon disappeared. For the first time in nearly 50 years, the march of commercial prosperity faltered at Guildford.

In the decade that followed, innumerable new projects were tried, all avenues of diversification were explored. Vehicles designed and developed included the Stork and Heron light trucks, aimed at competing with Albion's Claymore and Chieftain models. The Paravan appeared to offer something better than Austin-Morris's new FG for street delivery. The Fleet-Special van was built for newspaper work. The Pax range was developed with a 5½-litre Dennis diesel to compete with

Albion's Clydesdale, AEC's Mercury and Leyland's Comet. With the exception of the Pax, none of those projects went into volume production. Either they were too expensive, or too complex for the job they were to do, or often simply too long in getting from the prototype stage to production, by which time the opposition had soaked up the market demand.

However, there was still some very good engineering. The 0-6 engine had been bored out to 108 mm to produce 120 bhp, and was every bit as good as the Leyland 600 engine according to some bus engineers. The drop-centre axle of the Loline bus, and the U type and V type gearboxes used respectively in medium trucks and heavy buses, were among the best of their kind. But steadily, the Dennis system got left behind in the highly competitive technological and economic world of the 1950s and '60s. Too much fragmentation of effort had taken place, and the scale of production was too low to be an economical operation. By the late 1960s, production centred on fire engines and municipal vehicles, which by the very nature of their design and operation could not be made in large numbers. The Pax range and its derivatives like the Maxim continued in small quantities, while the bus business gradually faded away and ceased altogether in the late 1960s.

An ingenious and almost-successful truck range appeared in 1969, when a prototype tipper was exhibited at the tipper show at Buxton. It was a 10.5/11-ton payload (depending on body) machine, grossing at either 15.2 or 15.5 tons, depending on the version. That gave it the same payload as competitors' 16-tonners, but saved considerably on excise tax due to the low unladen and gross weight. It began life as the Pax V, and soon was renamed the DB15.5. So good was it that many operators, particularly in the tipper field, bought them and for a short while the Guildford production lines rang to the sounds of volume building of trucks. There was a 24-ton tractive unit called the DB24T or Defiant, using the turbocharged version of the Perkins 6.354 engine that powered the 15.5, and the same Dennis U type gearbox driving an Eaton axle. Together with a steady stream of municipal vehicles, particularly the Paxit series of continuous-loading refuse trucks, and a strong order book for fire engines, Dennis jogged along, but nobody pretended that it was anything like the company it had been before the war, or even in the 1950s.

Time had taken its toll, and once on that fatal treadmill, even the engineers of the calibre of Dennis's could not move quickly enough to get off again. In industrial Britain it was a familiar enough picture. The only solution, distasteful though it seemed at the time, was a takeover, for the prospects of continuing as an independent for much longer seemed slim. The first serious suitor was Harry Redmond, chairman of Seddon, who took a long hard look at Dennis in 1969. He eventually decided that the southern English temperament was not likely to mix well with his flinty northern attitude to life in general and work in particular, and he eventually went away and took over Atkinson instead. (See *World Trucks No 3, Seddon Atkinson*).

Shortly after Harry Redmond had gone back to Oldham, a new suitor appeared. That group liked what they saw at Guildford, and after a long repel-boarders action by the board of Dennis, which included some drastic reorganisation at company level, the new suitor, Hestair, finally won the day and acquired Dennis Brothers Ltd for £3.4 million which seemed a paltry sum considering the vast property and land holdings that Dennis boasted among its assets. The deal was signed early in 1972 and to many it seemed a black day at Guildford, but in the long run it turned out to be one of the best things that ever happened.

Principal Dennis engines, post White and Poppe

Type	Approx date	Bore and stroke		Output/rpm	Remarks
A,B,C,D	1931-on	100 x 120 mm	4-cyl	70/75 @ 3,000	petrol side valve
Light four	1951	100 x 120 mm	4-cyl	81.5 @ 3,000	petrol ohv
Big four	1931	116 x 150 mm	4-cyl	85 @ 2,600	petrol side valve
ohc six	1930	110 x 140 mm	6-cyl	100/105 @ 3,100	petrol ohc
0-4	1934	117.4 x 150 mm	4-cyl	80 @ 1,800	diesel dir inj
0-6	1937	105 x 146 mm	6-cyl	110 @ 2,000	diesel dir inj
0-6a	1947	108 x 146 mm	6-cyl	120 @ 2,000	diesel dir inj
0-6h	1951	108 x 146 mm	6-cyl	118 @ 2,000	horizontal version
Mk 1	1938	98 x 112 mm	6-cyl	75 @ 2,000	direct injection
Mk 2	1950	102 x 112 mm	6-cyl	93 @ 2,200	direct injection

There were several prototypes in addition to the above production units.

Principal Dennis gearboxes, 1930 onwards

Type	Speeds and concept	Remarks
L	4, sliding mesh	Originated 1929, numerous later versions
T4	4, constant mesh	Needle roller bearings, pump lubricated
T5	5, constant mesh	Needle roller bearings, pump lubricated
U	5, constant mesh	Simplified T, plain bearings, no pump
K	4, sliding mesh	Heavy duty, originated 1930, numerous versions
O	5, constant mesh	Mainly for Lancets, preselector overdrive
6/5	6 or 5, constant mesh	Indirect input-output line, full con-mesh including reverse
V4	4 or 5 constant mesh	Mainly for Lolines, very compact, very short selector
V5		movement, full constant mesh including reverse.

More than 3,000 Max 6-8 tonners were built during the years 1939-45 and saw service in all theatres of war, regarded with great affection by the army crews.

Left A special military version based on the Pax was developed in 1940-41 and around 2,000 were supplied mainly to the support arms of the forces, such as the Royal Corps of Signals, and the Royal Engineers.

Below Among the products during the war years were light gun carriers, with Ford engines, known as Lloyd Carriers. About 3,000 were built for infantry regiments.

Above Workers get a pep-talk in the yard at Woodbridge from a group of government and War Office officials in 1942.

Right Work on Churchill tanks in progress at Woodbridge during the 1939-45 war. Floors had to be strengthened in places to carry the weight.

Facing page The Jubilant high capacity six-wheeler was the first new model introduced after the war, and made its debut at the 1946 Trade Fair in Barcelona. It was a remarkably tough vehicle, rated at 19 tons gross and powered by the 0-6 engine.

Right The Max Major was an 18-ton, twin-steer chassis built mainly for the Yorkshire wool trade. This prototype is seen undergoing tests on the hills behind Guildford.

Below The post-war fire engine lineage was developed from the F1 but the F7, like this one, with Rolls-Royce petrol engine, was built in large numbers initially for London, but eventually for brigades all over the world.

Above In 1958 the Paravan was introduced as an attempt to build a safety-orientated city delivery vehicle. The driving position was cantilevered forwards, and the front access doors were angled at 45°.

Left The F28 fire engine was developed in 1958-59 primarily for London, but was widely used elsewhere. Rolls-Royce petrol engines were used, but soon after that, greater demand for diesel engines caused a steady switch to that fuel source.

Above Dennis appliances, among them a new F28, an F101 and the new hydraulic escape ladder, tackle a fire in Guildford in 1958.

Right In 1958 attempts to get the deck height down to speed unloading of cased drinks at public houses produced the Pax NC lowloader. Several brewers including Mackesons, Fremlins and Whitbreads used this type, which ran on 17-inch wheels.

TROUBLE AND STRIFE

Left One of the most successful brewer's drays was the Pax V low-deck six-wheeler which used 16-inch wheels with a tandem rear bogie. The load deck was only 40 inches above ground level. At least a dozen breweries used this model in the late 1960s.

Below left Lancet III bus chassis (left) and Pax normal control trucks were assembled side by side. This picture was taken in 1951.

Above right The Stork was a light-weight 2½-tonner built in the mid-1950s, to compete with vehicles like the Albion Claymore. It had a flat four-cylinder petrol engine.

Right Defiant was a name used more than once by Dennis. One was a front-engined bus chassis of the mid-1960s, but the 24-ton tractive unit, DB24T, was also called Defiant in 1973.

Below The Pax NC with its three man cab was always popular in jobs where there was a high labour content, such as beer delivery and, as seen here, timber handling.

Above A major step forward in refuse collection was the Paxit Major of 1952 which compressed domestic refuse to a quarter of its original volume. Local authorities all over Britain had fleets of P-Ms, and some of them still function.

Left and above right The Pax series of truck chassis which appeared from 1953 onwards continued for over ten years culminating in the highly successful Pax V. The pictures show a Pax IIa chassis with a gulley emptier body of 1954 and a Pax IV of 1957 with a demountable cattle body. Pax chassis were mainly Perkins 6.354-powered although a few early municipal models had Dennis 82 hp petrol engines.

Right Good weight distribution and smooth transmission were designed into Dennis ambulances to achieve good traction and safety under all road conditions.

Above The 1966 Earls Court Show stand majored on the new moulded two-piece glassfibre cabs on trucks, tractors and municipal vehicles.

Left A limited number of 22-ton 6 x 4 Pax V versions were built in the mid-1960s, with V8 Perkins engines. This version developed into the Maxim by 1966.

Above right The Pax was quite popular with specialist operators in businesses like agriculture and furniture because it was light. This Pax V had an 1,800 cu ft pantechnicon built on it in 1968.

Right The Tippax refuse vehicles of the mid- and late 1950s discharged the load by tipping.

Above The Paxit series which appeared from about 1961, ejected the load by an internal ram. The mechanism on the back compressed the refuse into the body and was lifted up for unloading. The picture shows a Paxit IIIA of 1965.

Left Dennis refuse systems included mechanical bin emptying for both the normal domestic bin and larger ones for hotels and industrial premises.

Right and below right Despite massive attacks on the UK bus markets from 1946 onwards by Leyland, AEC, Daimler, Crossley and Bristol, Dennis maintained a share of that market. Their local operator, Aldershot & District Traction Co had a big Dennis fleet, but loyal operators were found further afield, particularly in Lancashire, where Leigh Corporation and the Lancashire United Transport and Power Co operated Dennis fleets. The pictures show a Loline III in Guildford, an earlier Loline at Leigh and a Lance at LUT.

Below The post-war Lancet was a popular coach with good performance and low noise level. This Duple-bodied example worked with a Berkshire operator.

Background photograph A batch of Loline chassis leaves the works in 1958 on the way to the coachbuilders.

Inset Heavy Mercury tractors handled most of the world's aircraft including Concorde. Here a DC9 is being shunted at Heathrow.

Left Mercury industrial tractors were made in many sizes. Here an exported example services a KLM Super Constellation in Singapore. The Mercury operation was acquired by Dennis in 1964.

Below More than a dozen Dennis fire appliances attended this fire in a department store in Romford in 1972.

Above Limited numbers of 6 x 6 crash tenders were built by Dennis in the late 1960s and early '70s mainly for military airfields, to Air Ministry standards.

Right The Maxim 30-ton tractive unit with the Perkins V8-510 engine was introduced in 1966. That weight rating was rather ambitious for 165 hp, and the model was not popular.

Right The revolutionary front-wheel drive ambulance of 1971-72 had a 2.8-litre Jaguar engine, automatic transmission, a very low rear floor ideal for loading casualties, and independent suspension. Ambulance men loved it but their councils would not pay for it.

Top right and overleaf top The ultimate version of the Pax V was a 10.5/11-ton payload machine with the 110 bhp Perkins engine and U type Dennis gearbox. With minor changes this truck became the DB15.5 which went into line production in the winter of 1969-70. The low weight of this model was calculated to save about £68 a year on tax compared with a normal 16-tonner, with a comparable payload.

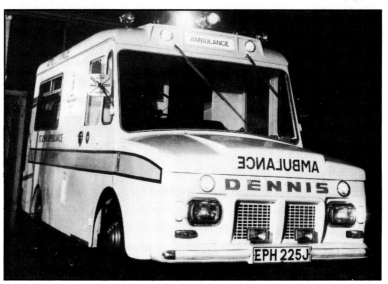

Right The Perkins T6.354 turbo-charged engine powered the DB24T Defiant, and proved to be a lively and economical unit.

Below left The DB15.5 of 1971 onwards was an 11-ton payload Perkins powered four-wheeler, though several were converted to 18-ton gross six-wheelers by the addition of a tag axle, like this one working near London.

Below The DB24T Defiant was one of the lightest and most economical 24-ton tractors in Britain in the early 1970s.

BACK FROM THE BRINK

When Hestair moved into Guildford, there were many traditionalists who threw their hands in the air and declared that things would never be the same again. They were right, but not in the way they thought. What Hestair did brought immediate cries of 'assets-strippers', or 'papermongers' from both inside and outside Dennis, and it must be admitted that on a short term basis those allegations looked justified. To begin with, all the land and property was sold off, leaving just a bare company structure — the hallmark of the asset stripper after a takeover. But looking at it deeper, Dennis needed a lot of cash spent on it to make it a viable company. The first balance sheet after the takeover showed a loss of nearly £1 million, and production was at an all-time low with semi-obsolete vehicles.

Hestair leased back the plant it needed from the company which had bought it, and the employees who lived in the innumerable company houses continued to live there but under a different landlord. From the cash so released, the job of rebuilding Dennis could begin. First of all the vehicles were updated to make them competitive. The continuous-loading refuse vehicle, for example, was replaced by a more economical intermittent loader. The decision was made to stop trying to compete in an already overcrowded UK truck market. That would need investment of many millions to produce the high-technology machines demanded by the market and the money clearly was not available. Instead, it was decided to concentrate on export markets where the kind of simple but highly reliable truck that Dennis could build would be accepted, namely the Mediterranean and Middle East.

The manufacture of sidelines like motor mowers and airfield tractors interrupted the all-important business of making trucks and municipals, so they were hived off, the mowers to Hestair's agricultural division still under the Dennis name, and the tractors to Marshalls of Halifax. New fire engine technology was developed, and a plant for the manufacture of tanks to be carried by the truck chassis for export was installed. It all took time to get together, but slowly it took shape. Those massive deficit figures began to melt away, and the word 'profit' was once again heard on the office floors at the front of the works.

The offices themselves in the meantime had changed. Gone were the marble stairs and mahogany corridors, and in their place modern, efficient installations including a computer for production and parts control. The marble is still there under the hall and stair carpet, and so are the D-B monograms. The company was by then named Dennis Motors Ltd, and traded by that name or Hestair-Dennis, depending on circumstances.

Two years went by before real profits emerged once again, but the new managing director was not complaining. His name was John Smith, and he kept very busy chasing up contacts and new orders throughout the Middle East, Mediterranean and north African areas, as well as the Far East. By the end of 1973 orders worth up to £1½ million at a time began to flow in from overseas. Two- and three-axle Delta-series trucks, the early ones with glassfibre cabs, later ones with steel, began to flow to the docks in convoys, on their way to places like Dubai, Libya, Cyprus, Saudi Arabia and Hong Kong. In the meantime, internal reorganisation had raised production to around 15 complete vehicles a week. That may not sound much but it should be remembered that a fire engine, for example, contains about five times as many man-hours as a simple chassis-cab. That was in 1975, and since then it has almost doubled again, to 28 a week.

By 1977, the recovery was well advanced. Turnover had reached an all-time record of £15 million for the financial year, from which a pre-tax profit of £1½ million emerged. Even the most anti-Hestair minds had to agree that the medicine had produced a cure, painful though it might have been for a short time. The workforce had been slimmed down by about 300, mainly through natural wastage, and production processes were made still more efficient. Both group assembly and flow-line systems were employed, the former mainly for all-different machines like fire engines, the latter for the export trucks, tankers and refuse vehicles. New projects were afoot too. Perhaps the most spectacular was the bus programme. Using a rationalised construction system, a rear-engined bus chassis for home markets and selected export markets, and a front-engined version for the wider export fields, was developed.

The philosophy behind that venture is important, There was no possibility of Dennis competing face to face in the UK bus market with the giant Leyland group, which offered four different models of double-decker alone, and even more single-deckers. What Dennis could offer, which the giants could not, was a tailor-made bus to suit a particular operator's exact needs, and in that they were successful. Some cities, Leicester in particular, ordered the Dominator, as it was called, in considerable quantity, and other users like West Yorkshire put it to work in their mixed fleets, where it gave a good account of itself. With production running at five a week, about half and half for export and home, and again half and half front- and rear-engined, the bus operation soon became big enough to contribute significantly to the profits, and that, after all, was what was required of it. The company won a Queen's Award for Exports in 1977 as a result of this activity, and the figures tell the story. Dennis exports rose from under half a million pounds in 1972 to £12.7 million in 1977. That was backed up by the *Sunday Times* Export Award presented by the Prime Minister early in 1978 for the best contribution from the workforce, and the Dennis party turned up at 10 Downing Street to collect their award in a Dominator double-decker.

At home new municipal vehicles including the ultra quiet and efficient Bulkmaster won larger shares of that particular market, and after the new R series fire engines were launched in 1976, Dennis succeeded in stepping up their share of that market, to the tune of over 400 machines a year. Birmingham took over a dozen of them in one delivery in 1976. The 1978 production programme included almost 2,000 vehicles, 75 per cent of those fully built up machines, and that volume produced a turnover of more than £20 million. It was not all plain sailing, however. After the boom years of the mid-1970s in the expanding markets of the Middle East, 1978 saw them settle down to a steady but small volume, and so large orders were hard to come by. Nevertheless, the forward order situation as 1979 began remained encouraging. A new steel tilt cab began production

early in 1979 which, with the Motor Panels steel cab, replaced glass fibre altogether. The Dennis cab, which embraced an ingeniously flexible tooling system, can be assembled in short or sleeper versions, different widths, and suitable for either fire engines, refuse vehicles, or trucks. It can also be a tilt or fixed version. However, the Motor Panels steel cab remains the principal fitment to export trucks, as distinct from fire or municipal chassis.

Following the tremendous export successes of the mid-1970s, and the successful re-entry into both the domestic and export bus markets in 1977-78, Dennis re-entered the domestic truck market right at the end of 1978. The Hestair-Dennis board, heartened by those successes, and by those of their municipal vehicles and fire engines in Great Britain, commissioned a modified version of the Delta-2 chassis for domestic sale and, by the New Year of 1979, a chain of distributors was established to handle the domestic Dennises.

The policy at Hestair-Dennis is to remain fully flexible while keeping to the strict requirements of specific export markets demanding long life sturdy vehicles, and a home market wanting special attentions not available from the big groups. That formula in a highly competitive world makes the company unique, and as such it is assured of a place among the world's truck builders, even though the production levels are only a few per cent of those of the biggest European names. In the words of the managing director, 'You don't have to be big to be successful in trucks. All you have to do is be clever enough to find the right slots in the market, and flexible enough to fill them.'

Dennis profits were spectacular in the mid-1920s and a steady growth after the Depression of the 1930s right through to 1955 reflected a secure situation at Guildford. But thereafter performance was erratic up to the takeover early in 1972 by the Hestair group.

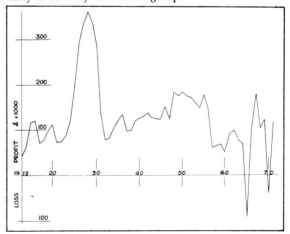

DENNIS

Left The Firebird was a water carrier with a simple pump at the rear, intended for supplying water to fires in export markets where there was limited mains access.

Below Steel-cab Delta chassis in four- and six-wheeled versions comprised the bulk of Dennis's export business to the Middle East and Africa.

BACK FROM THE BRINK

Right Soon after the completion of development of the rear-engined Dominator in 1977, examples began to appear in export markets, notably in Hong Kong. This picture was taken there in 1978.

Right A Delta III tanker goes aboard ship at Southampton en route for a Middle Eastern military customer. Perkins V8 640 engines power these machines.

Below Gardner 6LXB engine and Voith gearbox installation across the rear of the Dominator chassis.

Background photograph One of the most successful fire appliances in Dennis's long history was the R type, introduced in 1976, and seen here on trial at Oulton Park motor racing circuit.

Inset One of the highly successful export chassis, on which Dennis's spectacular recovery of the mid-1970s was based, was the Waterbird—a tanker vehicle for use in semi-desert territories. Like most models from Guildford then, it used a Perkins 354-series engine with the 540 as an alternative, and carried the Dennis grp cab.

In 1978 a Rolls-Royce powered Dominator was added to West Yorkshire's fleet at Sheffield, on trials with competing makes. Most Dominators were fitted with Gardner engines.